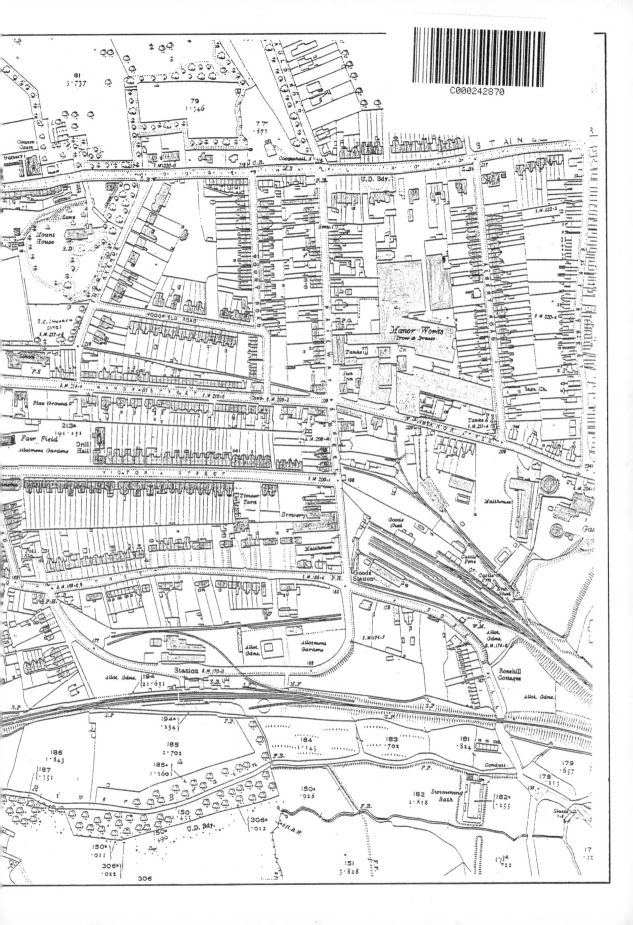

BRAINTREE & BOCKING

A Pictorial History

This copy engraving shows the High Street, *c*.1850, looking towards Chelmsford. The colonnaded building on the left is the Corn Exchange, built in 1839. Like so many other buildings of character in the town, it was demolished in post-war years despite public protests.

BRAINTREE & BOCKING
A Pictorial History

John Marriage

Phillimore

1994

Published by
PHILLIMORE & CO. LTD.,
Shopwyke Manor Barn, Chichester, West Sussex

ISBN 0 85033 909 X

Printed and bound in Great Britain by
BIDDLES LTD.
Guildford, Surrey

Dedicated to my wife, Marion Marriage,
who spent much of her childhood
at Braintree.

List of Illustrations

Frontispiece: The High Street, *c.*1840

Acknowledgements

The author wishes to thank the following for permission to reproduce photographs and illustrations: David Boutell, 47-49; Braintree & Bocking Heritage Trust (Alfred Whybrow collection), frontispiece, 7, 15, 25, 26, 31-33, 35, 37, 54-56, 60-62, 65-68, 86-90, 99, 110, 113, 114, 116-21, 126, 128-31, 139-44, 148, 152-55, 162, 168, 169, 171; Chelmsford Star Co-operative Society Ltd., 50, 51, 84, 150, 173; Crittall Windows Ltd., 10, 69, 70-74, 93, 127, 164; Essex Police, 97, 111, 112, 170; Ruby Goodwin, 52, 53, 78, 94, 95, 109, 135, 156, 163, 165-67, 172, 174, 177; Rita Harris, 178; Brian Joscelyne, 1, 159, 160; Melvyn Joscelyne, 2, 9, 18, 24, 34, 38-41, 58, 85, 91, 92, 96, 133, 143, 158; Tim Lake, 75, 79-83; Lloyds Bank plc, 59; Susan Mitchell, 137, 138; NatWest, 4, 57; Alan Osborne, 100-7; James Townrow, 5, 18, 36, 42, 45, 46. The remainder are from the author's collection.

In preparing this book I have received considerable help from a large number of people and organisations. I would like especially to thank Adam Smith of Braintree Museum, Brian Joscelyne for introducing me to a number of sources of information, including his cousin, Melvyn Joscelyne, as well as providing me with various illustrations. In addition Mrs. Ruby Goodwin, David Boutell and James Townrow all loaned me various items of Braintree memorabilia. Finally, but not least, I must also thank my wife who cheerfully corrected the grammatical and spelling errors and made invaluable suggestions on the contents.

Foreword

Braintree and Bocking were once quite separate communities which slowly merged into a single unit. The founding of Braintree was quite sudden, being created by the Bishop of London nearly 800 years ago as a planned 'new town'. Bocking developed more modestly as a rural community with links to the wool trade. These separate beginnings make a physical impact even today, some 60 years after the two townships finally became one in the rather disjointed road pattern and the subsequent lack of integration between the expanding suburbs.

Braintree was the main market town for north-west Essex and, with Bocking, became the home for important manufacturers. The first to arrive was wool and then silk weaving. Heavy engineering arrived in the last century. These industries grew to world wide acclaim, providing employment and comparative wealth for the inhabitants. Sadly, in the second half of the present century there has been some decline and painful adjustment. Both the livestock and arable markets are no more and the major industries have mostly gone. Many of the factories have been demolished. Local retailers are having to cope with the opposition and greater choice offered by the larger shopping complexes at Chelmsford and Colchester. Although an attractive new shopping precinct has been opened, many of the shopkeepers have merely relocated themselves from older premises, leaving them vacant. To improve competitiveness the centre has been pedestrianised and traffic removed by the surgically created Pierrefitte Way; its scars are yet to heal.

Increasingly, residents work elsewhere. A growing number commute daily to London by rail or road and it seems that this trend is likely to continue and be supplemented by employment in the new service industries growing up around Stansted Airport. Braintree's role as a commuter town is likely to grow.

In meeting local people I have been repeatedly told that 'Braintree has been spoilt' and certainly it has suffered from unfeeling development in the 1960s and '70s, robbing the town of some of its individuality. Nevertheless, many old buildings of considerable interest remain and there are encouraging signs that there is now a greater appreciation of the town's heritage, perhaps spearheaded by the setting up of the Braintree Museum in one of the town's best loved buildings.

In this book I have gathered together pictures from Victorian times to the middle of the present century showing Braintree and Bocking before the decline of so many local enterprises and when it was a still a self-contained Essex country town.

Chapter 1

Introduction

Braintree and Bocking were once two entirely separate communities but have long since fused into a single town. Indeed, at an early date the built up area of the town extended over the two separate civil parishes. The first known settlement in the vicinity lay on the clay capped ridge between the Rivers Brain and Pant, at that point only a mile apart where there was a crossing of east and west Stane Street with another Roman road from Chelmsford (Caesaromagus) towards the north east. In Roman times Stane Street was of considerable importance as it ran between Colchester (Camulodunum), initially the capital of Roman England, and St Albans (Verulamium), as well as Watling Street and Ermine Street, two of the great national routes from London (Londinium). Although of lesser importance, the route through Chelmsford was also well used as it gave direct access from London northwards via a settlement at Long Melford to East Anglia.

Prior to the Roman period, there was an Iron Age settlement nearby and traces of earthworks survived until recently in the grounds of Mount House. During the Roman occupation a small community developed at the intersection of the two roads and substantial quantities of coin have been found in the vicinity. The site was probably abandoned when the Romans left. The modern founding of Braintree was in 1199 when the Bishop of London established a small town close to the intersection of the two roads simultaneously with one at Chelmsford. It has been suggested from the topography that the Bishop intended to reproduce an identical ground plan to that of Chelmsford and certainly there are many similiarities, even though the site lacks the confluence of two rivers. Bocking grew up along the Sudbury Road, where even now in Bradford Street there are very fine medieval houses. Its special assets were the weirs and mills of the River Pant (upper Blackwater).

The name Braintree originally referred only to the Bishop of London's site and initially it was a minor community in the larger manor of Great Rayne, owned by the Bishop. The centre of this holding, which included an episcopal palace and grange, was a mile to the south east of the present town centre, at what is now Chapel Hill. Traces of these structures existed until the last century but disappeared under factories and warehouses.

In medieval times and the middle ages, Braintree was an important stopover for travellers from the Midlands proceeding to the Low Countries and to pilgrims from southern England visiting the shrine of St Edmund at Bury St Edmunds and that of Our Lady of Walsingham, though this activity was reduced by the Reformation. At the time of the Black Death in 1665 the town suffered a major setback, when a third of the population died. Weaving was first established in the 14th century and augmented by Flemish emigrés who settled here after fleeing the Low Countries as a result of religious persecution. Later, George Courtauld—himself descended from Huguenots, moved his silk business from neighbouring Pebmarsh in 1809.

In 1834, just prior to the construction of the railways, there were four licensed stage coaches passing through Braintree from London (40 miles) and Chelmsford (12 miles) to Bury St Edmunds and beyond. Overnight accommodation and a change of horses were provided there. In addition, there were local coaches to Colchester (15 miles), Bishops Stortford, Clare, Hedingham and Yeldham, together with regular carrier services to London, Colchester, Chelmsford, and Bishops Stortford. All these activities enhanced the town's trade.

The prosperity of the weaving and silk industry together with the later establishment of rapidly expanding engineering firms, like Crittalls and Lake & Elliot, resulted in a steady increase in the population of the town. In 1849 it comprised some 4,000 people. A hundred years later, in 1951, it had risen to 17,520, though by that date there was already a substantial amount of commuting between workers living in the neighbouring towns of Chelmsford, Braintree, Halstead, Witham and Maldon proceeding to and from the various factories. A substantial number of Braintree workers in those days were employed in the then thriving Marconi, Crompton and Hoffmann factories at Chelmsford.

Today, the original street pattern established for the little town by the Bishop of London nearly 800 years ago still survives although over the centuries the buildings flanking High Street, Bank Street and Great Square have been mostly rebuilt several times. However, many of considerable age still remain. The centre was pedestrianised in 1993 and the once extensive livestock market, originally held in the Great Square, High Street and Bank Street and more latterly in covered accommodation on the present site of Tesco's, has gone. All that remains of Braintree's former importance as a market town are the thriving retail stalls in the town centre. Sadly, too, the important landmarks of the Corn Exchange and the *Horn Hotel* have also disappeared, though the structure of the latter remains.

Braintree has links with a sister town overseas. In 1626, the Rev. Hooker who had previously preached at St Mary's (now the Cathedral) at Chelmsford, moved to Braintree where he lectured in the market place on puritanism, eventually establishing the Braintree Company. In 1632 most of the Company set sail for America in the ship *Lyon* and they eventually established the New England town of Braintree.

Chapter 2

Residential

Until early post-war years the original legacy of dwelling houses survived almost intact at both Braintree and Bocking. Clustered around the original settlement at High Street and Bank Street were a substantial number of typical East Anglian-style timber-framed and rendered cottages, mainly built in terraces and often close to the road but with some garden space immediately at the rear. Many were once occupied by weavers. Further from the centre were newer artisan's houses which sprang up to serve the rapidly expanding engineering factories, they were mostly tiny and cramped with little or no garden space. Later development, built after the passing of the Public Health Acts of the 1880s, show some improvement, although the long straight roads and terraces effectively ironed out all the natural features. Houses remained small, consisting of a small parlour and sitting room and kitchen on the ground floor, with two or three bedrooms upstairs. Sanitary arrangements were sparse, with a cold water tap in the kitchen and outside water closet. Earlier this century the first council houses were built mainly on the periphery of the town and continued through into the '50s and '60s. Substantial numbers of private houses were also built in the inter-war period. Larger detached houses were built along the approach roads to the town, like Oaklands, later White Courts, in London Road and in roads such as 'The Avenue'. Although later considered ugly, an important step in the construction of working class housing took place in 1919 when the first flat-roofed houses in the country were built by Crittall's in Cressing Road, using prefabricated parts. The experience gained by the Company in this work was very valuable when they proceeded with the construction of the garden village at Silver End, one of the most advanced town planning schemes of its day.

Town Centre

1. This fascinating aerial photograph of the town centre, *c*.1955, was taken prior to the present familiar features like The George Yard shopping precinct and Pierrefitte Way. Tesco's had yet to displace the livestock market and Sainsbury's was yet to appear behind The Great House in Tofts Walk.

2. The High Street, looking towards Chelmsford, *c*.1900. *Horn Hotel* is on the left, with a glimpse of the cobbled entrance to the yard behind. Beyond is the Corn Exchange with its useful clock. This attractive building was demolished earlier this century. The clock, however, has been transferred to the replacement building.

3. Looking up the High Street towards the Bank Street/Great Square junction, around 1930. Foster Brothers, the outfitters, then occupied the prominent corner site, hence Fosters Corner. Their premises are now occupied by the Midland Bank.

4. The substantial buildings marking the High Street/Bank Street junction, c.1900. Both buildings survive although considerable changes have been made to the ground-floor level. The bank premises have been converted into small shops, whilst the entrance to The George Yard shopping precinct has been driven through the other building.

5. Bank Street, looking towards the White Hart junction, *c*.1900. In those days it was a very narrow road through to the junction. It was broadened by the acquisition of Dr. Jack Harrison's garden, and various other properties, some demolished as a result of war damage.

6. Bank Street, *c*.1938, looking towards High Street. The broad area in the foreground was created by incorporating Dr. Jack Harrison's garden into the highway. Previously the road passed on both sides of his land, creating a leafy island.

7. Bocking End, looking towards Convent Bridge, c.1925. On the left is Braintree & West Essex Co-operative's main store, then only eight years old and a mecca for shoppers after their 'divi'.

8. White Hart corner as seen from Bank Street, c.1905, looking towards Bocking End. For centuries the hotel (right) has dominated the entrance to the town from Rayne Road (Stane Street). The old Roman highway continues as Coggeshall Road on the right of the hotel.

9. New Street in 1910 was once one of the busiest and most notorious streets in the town. One hundred years ago there were three pubs near its junction with Great Square—*The Three Tuns*, *The George* and the *Green Man*, respectively known as 'Little Hell', 'Great Hell' and 'Damnation'. All were eventually incorporated into Joscelyne's Furniture Stores. Previously, *The George* had been a lodgings known as 'The Workman's Rest'. In this picture, the ironwork across the street which once sported the pub sign still survives. Today the buildings are in retail use.

10. George Yard as it appeared in 1900, then with only a narrow entrance from Bank Street via a gant (alleyway). Francis Crittall started his engineering business in the buildings on the right, eventually encroaching onto the alleyway, before moving to a purpose-built factory in Manor Street. Today, the same buildings have been refurbished and are part of the present George Yard shopping precinct.

11. Rayne Road, looking towards the Bank Street junction, c.1910. The Victorian Gothic structure is the Methodist Church, opened in 1868. Built to accommodate a congregation of 450, it had a Manse and Sunday school adjoining. The church was demolished in 1988 to make way for the George Yard precinct. The school and Manse were removed in 1937 to allow the Braintree Co-operative Society to extend their premises.

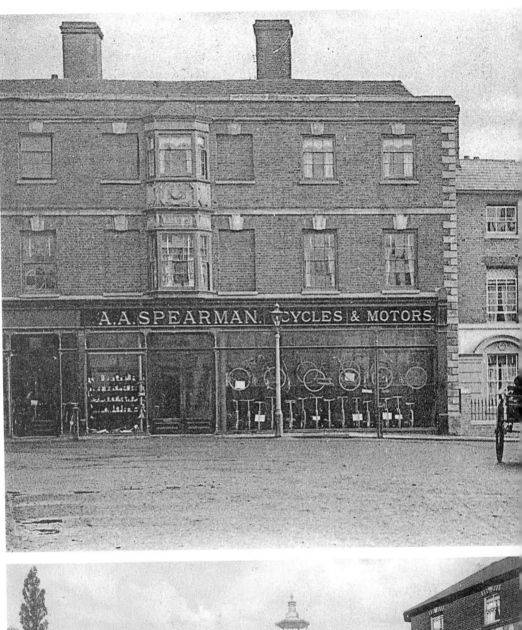

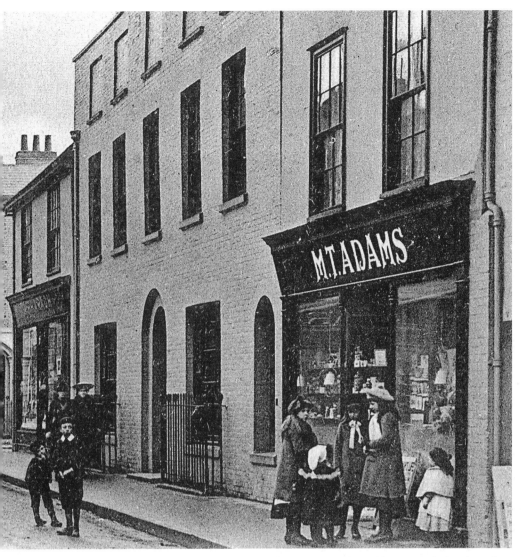

12. Great Square, *c*.1900. The listed Great House (facing), is an impressive 16th-century timber-framed building with an 18th-century red brick front. In 1900 the ground floor was a shop selling cycles, then one of the most popular forms of transport. Today, much of the premises are occupied by the old established Constitutional Club with the earlier red brick front substantially restored.

13. A quiet day at the Market Place, *c*.1910. The drinking fountain was presented to the town by George Courtauld M.P. in 1882. The *Nags Head* public house can be seen on the right of the picture, and *The Bull* public house is on the far side of the square. On market day the open area was crammed with penned sheep and cattle as well as stalls and farm waggons, but today only a few retail stalls and parked cars can be seen.

14. St Michael's church, High Street, *c*.1950. The large square and fountain were designed by John Hodge, the sculptor, and were given to the town by Sir W. J. Courtauld in memory of King George V.

The Environs

15. Twyford House, Rayne Road, *c.*1895, a beautiful Georgian town mansion, where reputedly John Bunyan stayed, dominates the road near the *White Hart*. More recently, the electricity board took over the building and inserted a shop front at ground floor level. They have now moved to George Yard so the future of this building is uncertain.

16. Rayne Road, *c*.1900, looking westwards to its junction with Panfield Lane. The small gable-ended structure in the centre is Lake & Elliot's original Albion Works which they occupied before moving to new premises at Chapel Hill.

17. Rayne Road, *c*.1905. At the turn of the century these attractive timber framed and plastered terraced cottages faced undeveloped land. It is thought that some were occupied by silk outworkers and the south facing windows would have provided good light. Today they are close to the busy Pierrefitte Way junction.

18. 'Lyton', London Road, built by Francis Crittall, *c*.1905, complete with metal windows of his own design.

19. London Road, *c*.1905, was then a quiet peaceful road. On the reverse of the postcard is written, 'I am staying in this road'. The writer would probably have been appalled at the noise created by today's busy junction and insensitive layout with Pierrefitte Way.

20. Another view of London Road, *c*.1900, looking from the railway bridge away from the town, over the now derelict Dunmow line, towards Chelmsford.

21. Coggeshall Road, *c*.1900. The timber-faced house on the right was once occupied by Dr. Jack Harrison's gamekeeper. 'Dr. Jack' named it Brigand Cottage after a lucky win on the horses. Beyond is the County Court, currently occupied as a public library, pending the construction of a new building in Fairfield Road.

22. This attractive terrace of thatched cottages still survives in Cressing Road, seen here *c*.1910. Originally they were encompassed by open farmland. Today, they are somewhat incongruously surrounded by urban development.

23. The Avenue, *c*.1915, was then one of the more fashionable places to live. Substantially built Victorian houses overlooked the arboreal grounds of Mount House.

24. The interior of a prosperous Braintree house in the late 1930s. It was furnished entirely by Joscelyne's in the fashionable style of the times. The large bay window was made from Crittall standard metal frames.

25. Before the railway came, Notley Road was one of the busiest roads into the town and a turnpike carrying goods to and from the important port of Maldon. By the time this picture was taken, c.1910, it had become a quiet lane into the town flanked by artisans' cottages.

26 & 27. Two views showing the Notley Road crossing of the River Brain, near Rifle Hill, *c*.1910. For most of the year it is only a small stream but after heavy rain the road was liable to flood. A board walk and railings were provided for pedestrians use but horse-drawn traffic had to traverse the swollen waters. In picture 26 a summer flood brings the children to the water.

28. Bradford Street, Bocking, *c*.1915, has many large medieval timber-framed buildings of great character fronting the hill winding down towards the River Blackwater. Many are listed as well as being part of an Outstanding Conservation Area. It is undoubtedly the most attractive street in the town.

29. The lower end of Bradford Street, *c*.1920, flanked by smaller workers' cottages. Although it is the main road to Halstea and Sudbury, traffic in those days was very light.

30. The Franciscan Convent and Broad Road, as seen from the bridge over the River Blackwater, *c.*1910. It was then on the edge of open countryside whereas today there is now a ribbon of houses almost as far as the new bypass.

31. Church Street, Bocking, *c.*1900. In the centre is the Church Street branch of the Braintree & West Essex Co-operative Society. It opened about 1880 as part of a rapid expansion of the society in the town and outlying areas.

32. Church Street, Bocking, c.1910. The Courtauld family, in addition to making substantial philanthropic gifts to the community, also built in 1872 a number of workmen's cottages, seen here on the right. They were substantially and attractively built to a standard well in advance of their times. An employee, Tam Whybrow, watches the camera with interest.

33. These picturesque white plastered thatched cottages, seen here c.1920, once occupied land next to the United Reformed church in Church Street, Bocking. Post-war council-built bungalows now occupy the site.

Chapter 3

Commerce

Like most market towns on former coaching routes, Braintree had a wealth of public houses in Victorian times, providing the only liquid refreshment which was both safe and relatively cheap as well as providing convivial company. Most were of ancient origin. Their number has fallen steadily throughout this century and many have been either demolished or converted to other uses as trade declined with the expansion of alternative forms of entertainment. The growth of television in post-war years has had a particularly adverse affect, resulting in people remaining at home in the evenings. The best known survivor is the *White Hart*, a particularly attractive hotel standing at the junction of Bank Street with Bocking End.

Some of the brews were produced locally, like Youngs of Railway Street and Ridleys in Manor Road. Others came from further afield like Wells & Perry of Chelmsford or Greene King from Bury St Edmunds.

The Victorian era saw the establishment of the modern banking system and branches of national banks began to be opened in the town. The earliest was Sparrow and Company, who arrived in the town in 1803 and later joined forces with other local banks to become part of the so-called Essex Bank. Later, it was taken over by Barclays, who still occupy the same building in Bank Street. Lloyds Bank arrived nearby in 1920, converting an existing rather dignified Victorian building into their local branch. Twenty years later the building was totally destroyed by a direct hit during an enemy air raid. The present building, together with adjacent shops, also replacing those destroyed, was not opened until October 1958. Interestingly, a display case inside contains Roman pottery found whilst the foundations were being excavated. Unfortunately, the new buildings, although not ugly, were built to a conventional 1950s London suburban style, which really do not reflect the character of an old Essex market town.

Like Chelmsford, Braintree was originally established as a trading town, with its market charter granted by King John in 1199. The original market was apparently in the area between Great Square, Bank Street, Drury Lane and the *Swan Hotel*. However, over the years, as in many other towns, the stalls were replaced by permanent structures, built of lath and plaster over a timber frame. Many of these have only been demolished within the last few years. Between these buildings narrow alleyways, known locally as 'Gants', were retained, providing access and short cuts. Examples are Leather Lane and Iremonger (or Ironmonger) Lane. Even today, although reduced in number, the town centre is unique in the continued existence of these alleyways.

In 1631, as a result of the growth of trade, the market moved to a larger site in what became known as New Market Street, later simply New Street. This became one of the busiest areas in the town. However, the market continued to occupy the Market Place, Bank Street and High Street.

High Street, Bank Street and adjoining areas have long been the centre for retail trade with many of the properties converted from private houses. Today, most of the shops are branches of national chain stores but earlier this century almost all of them were owned by individual proprietors who either lived above the premises, or, if they were sufficiently prosperous and successful, in villas close by or in one of the nearby villages. The shops catered for the total needs of the local community. As well as tailors, chemists, drapers and grocers etc., the shops represented trades such as hatters and coopers. One of the longest established firms was the well known furnishing business of Henry Joscelyne Ltd. It was started towards the end of the 18th century by Benjamin Joscelyne, who took over an existing business and later moved into a former High Street inn—the *White Hart*—facing up Bank Street, now 62 High Street. This was subsequently enlarged by taking in 60 High Street as well as premises in New Street and the whole was substantially rebuilt. Uniquely, as well as operating the furniture business, Benjamin also undertook auction sales and, later, property sales. Eventually, the two businesses became separated and the present firm of Joscelyne & Sons, Estate Agents, moved into their offices in Bank Street in 1961. Sadly, the furnishing business, once one of the most respected in Essex, closed in 1981, although the building survives. Another substantial local retailer was the Braintree Co-operative Society Ltd. This was formed in 1864 as the Braintree and West Essex Co-operative Society Ltd. by a number of local weavers, taking as their model a similar society which had earlier been established in Colchester. Their first store was in a small cottage in Pound Lane. This was quickly found to be inadequate and within 15 months arrangements had been made to rent a small shop in Swan Street. The Society grew rapidly and towards the end of the century they had established their main central premises in Bocking End, subsequently to be rebuilt and enlarged. Branches were established on various sites and a coal and milk business started. Various social activities were organised. In 1964 the Society had a membership of 9,633 persons, a total of 21 shops and departments, 180 employees, a fleet of 36 vehicles, including 6 mobile shops and an annual trade of £650,000, in those days a substantial sum. Unfortunately, the subsequent years were not kind to small independent co-operative societies and in the 1980s the Society was taken over by the larger and more dynamic Chelmsford Society. Under their banner 'Quadrant' their Rayne Road premises have been rebuilt and vastly expanded to become one of the largest and most attractive shops in Braintree, incorporated within the George Yard shopping precinct.

The 1930s and the '40s were the golden age of the silver screen, when 'going to the pictures' was a weekly event for most people. There were two cinemas in Braintree: The Embassy, in Fairfield Road, and The Central, in High Street. An earlier cinema known as The Palace previously occupied the site of The Embassy, which replaced it in the 1930s. Its future appears doubtful as film patrons seem to be drawn to multi-screen cinemas at Chelmsford and Colchester. Its namesake at Maldon, also owned by the Shipman and King group, was demolished in the 1980s and a shop now occupies the site of The Central.

Commerce

34. No book on Braintree would be complete without a copy of this impression of High Street in 1826, depicting many of the street sellers, hawkers and local gentry.

35. Market day, High Street, *c*.1900. A miscellaneous collection of items are for sale, including farm implements and rolls of carpet. Coming up the road is a flock of sheep. The *Horn Hotel* seems to be doing good business and the local butcher has a fine selection of carcasses hanging outside his shop.

36. The once busy *Orange Tree Inn*, in the Market Place, *c*.1905. Spectators gather by the livestock pens. The inn was demolished in 1957 and replaced by a modern building of similar size and now occupied by a dry cleaner's.

37. Market Place, *c*.1900. In its prime Braintree market was always bustling with activity. There were sheep, cattle and horses for sale, merchandise to be moved and deals to be struck amid the general hubbub. In the distance is Balls & Balls Cattle Market, now replaced by Tesco's supermarket. Closer and still surviving is *The Bull* public house. The harness maker's premises next door is now a shop.

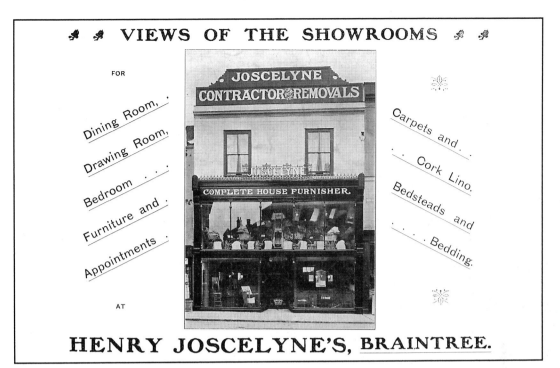

VIEWS OF THE SHOWROOMS

FOR

Dining Room, .

Drawing Room,

Bedroom . . .

Furniture and :

Appointments .

AT

JOSCELYNE
CONTRACTOR REMOVALS

COMPLETE HOUSE FURNISHER.

Carpets and . .

. . Cork Lino.

Bedsteads and

. . . . Bedding.

HENRY JOSCELYNE'S, BRAINTREE.

38. A copy of Henry Joscelyne's advertisement for his substantial furnishing business in High Street, *c*.1900.

39. Joscelyne's was one of the earliest 'walk round' stores where customers were invited to browse. On display are various items for the bedroom. The wardrobe mirror reflects for posterity a passing horse and cart, *c*.1905.

40. Henry Joscelyne's extensive lino and carpet selection, the largest in Braintree, *c*.1905.

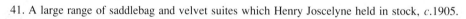

41. A large range of saddlebag and velvet suites which Henry Joscelyne held in stock, *c*.1905.

42. Charles Townrow's premises at The Red House, 42 Bank Street, around 1915. In those days trousers were fashioned to a 'wholefall' pattern, an alternative to the present means of fastening.

43. Foster Bros. advertise their 1936 'back to school' sale in the *Essex Chronicle*. They specialised in selling school clothes at economical prices from a shop at the Bank Street/High Street corner, hence Fosters Corner. Midland Bank now occupy the site and Fosters have moved elsewhere.

44. The *Essex Chronicle* advertisement appeared in 1936 announcing the 15th birthday sale of Joys, a popular ladies shop which originated in Colchester and had branches in both Chelmsford and Braintree. They closed during the post-war years.

45. This extract from a *c.*1910 Charles Townrow catalogue gives some idea of how men's styles have changed, even though the Covert Coat looks quite familiar.

46. The interior of Charles Townrow's outfitter's shop about 1910. In those days shops always provided chairs for the customers as a matter of courtesy, a habit which could usefully be revived today.

47. James Bowtell's original family grocery premises at 60 High Street, *c*.1900. James Bowtell (centre) is flanked by Wiggy Brown (*left*) and Fred Atkins (*right*). Bowtell's later moved to Bank Street and closed as recently as 1994. The original premises were demolished to make way for an extension to Henry Joscelyne's store.

48. James Bowtell's later double-fronted shop in Bank Street, *c.*1925. During the post-war years the shop was reduced to a single front.

49. The interior of James Bowtell's grocery shop at 31 Bank Street, *c.*1925. Frank Godfrey, seen here, remained with the firm for his entire working life, 1923-85.

50 & 51. The Braintree & West Essex Co-operative Society Ltd. was founded in 1864 by a small group of working men in this small weaver's cottage in South Street. Their first shop was in Pound Lane but they quickly moved to a larger building in Swan Street, the premises occupied by the fishmongers and probably also those of S. Watts, illustrated below. This in turn was replaced by premises in Bocking End in 1875.

52. Lawrence & Goodwin's wet fish shop in Cressing Road in 1933.

53. In 1936 L. Goodwin ran a high quality fish and chip shop in Rayne Road. A few customers visited the premises by car but most walked or cycled. Today, this family business still carries on elsewhere in the town.

54. The Misses E. Osborn stand outside their fancy goods shop in Bank Street, *c*.1930.

55. Albert Pilgrim poses outside his greengrocery shop in New Street together with his assistant Miss D. Watson, *c*.1922. Greengrocers have always displayed their wares outside and this tradition has changed little over the years. Prices, though, are beyond recognition.

56. In 1898 Albert Spearman's shop in Market Place was a popular meeting place for cycling enthusiasts. Cycling was an essential form of transport for ordinary people as well as a cheap method of recreation. Cycles came in all shapes and sizes from ordinary two wheelers to racers, tricycles, tandems, invalid carriages and delivery bikes. Spearman later moved to larger premises in Great House in Great Square.

57. The modern banking system has evolved over the years with many amalgamations and mergers. At the turn of the century the present premises of Nat West was occupied by The London County Westminster & Parr's bank, one of its predecessor companies.

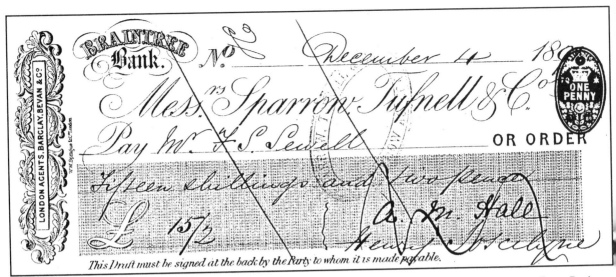

58. Copy of a Sparrow, Tufnell & Co's cheque issued in December 1891. This bank was also known as the Essex Bank and was eventually taken over by Barclays who still occupy the same premises in Bank Street.

59. In the early post-war years Britain struggled back to normality as best it could. The bombed site in Bank Street remained vacant for some years but Lloyds Bank quickly erected a temporary hut and re-established normal business until a building licence could be sought to construct the present bank chamber.

Chapter 4

Industry

Weaving was first established in the area in the 14th century when a type of heavy East Anglian broadcloth, a form of rough twill, was produced. During the Elizabethan period the local weavers were joined by an influx of Flemish refugees, fleeing from Spanish persecution in the Netherlands. They introduced new techniques which enabled a lighter cloth to be woven. This became known as 'Bockings'.

After the Revocation of the Edict of Nantes in 1685 some 400,000 French Protestants—the Huguenots—fled France and took refuge in other countries. Many of them were silk weavers and some settled in Spitalfields. Towards the end of the 18th century a Huguenot descendant, George Courtauld, became apprenticed to a silk throwster—a worker who twists silk thread into yarn—at Spitalfields. He later moved to Pebmarsh where he set up his own silk factory. Then in 1810 he moved to larger premises at Braintree. The raw silk, mostly Bengali, Chinese or Italian, was brought by carrier from London. However, the mill was not a great success and it was his son Samuel who was the real founder of the Courtauld business. In 1816 he opened a small factory at Bocking for the manufacture of silk yarn. Later he was joined by two brothers and a brother-in-law and together they steadily expanded the business with employees migrating to Braintree from the surrounding villages, London and elsewhere. Later, the firm moved into the manufacture of artificial silk, with Rayon and Nylon becoming renowned throughout the world. From being a major local employer, Courtaulds developed into a huge international combine. Sadly however, although Courtauld is still a household name, it no longer has any local factories.

Another well-known local silk weaving firm was Warner & Son of New Mills. Like Courtaulds, this firm also originated at Spitalfields and moved to Braintree in 1895, taking over premises previously occupied by Daniel Walters & Sons, who had been silk weavers in the town since the 1820s and had established a reputation for the manufacture of high quality silk furnishing fabrics. Warner & Sons continued to produce both luxurious and practical fabrics. It had the distinction of supplying the material for both the coronation robe of King George VI and the bridal train for Queen Elizabeth II. Further work was carried out for Queen Elizabeth's Coronation in 1953 and the investiture of the Prince of Wales in 1969. Following a contraction in their market, Warners ceased to weave in Braintree in 1971 and scrapped all their power looms. However, some of the old hand looms and other machinery were rescued by Richard Humphries, and part of New Mills is now back in use as a working silk museum. It is open to the public six days a week and visitors are able to gain an insight into the production of silk, examples of which they can purchase.

Lake & Elliot was founded in 1892 by Mr. W. B. Lake in small premises in New Street as a manufacturer of a few specialities for the then thriving bicycle trade, employing three or four men. Four years later he was joined by Mr. E. F. Elliot and they worked in premises known as Albion Works, in Rayne Road. The firm rapidly expanded to some 25 persons making tools and accessories for the cycle trade, together with jacks for the developing automobile industry. In the next few years they gradually enlarged the scope of their business whilst becoming specialists in the construction of a wide variety of vehicle jacks. In 1905 they built an iron foundry in Chapel Hill for the production of iron castings and the following year a steel foundry which led to the production of very high quality steel castings with a total workforce of about 120 men. When the First World War broke out the firm had already built an electric furnace, so making it possible to further expand production. By then, they had a work force of 150 men and were able to move over rapidly to war production, executing many orders for both the Admiralty and the War Office. This included the production of fuses, which were supplied to the Royal Arsenal at Woolwich. During the Second World War the company again turned to war work, making components for tanks, warships, aircraft and other military vehicles. Jacks were supplied for fighting vehicles of all kinds as well as for ARP work. The firm's international reputation grew. Latterly it also made pressure castings and special fittings for North Sea oil rigs. Unfortunately, like so many old established engineering firms in Essex and East Anglia in recent years, the factory was taken over and closed.

Crittall Windows Ltd. also had humble beginnings with the purchase in 1864 of an ironmongery business in Bank Street by F. B. Crittall. This expanded into a warehouse facing George Yard, where a range of general engineering activities was undertaken. His son, Francis, eventually took over the business which he continually expanded particularly relating to metalwork. His small firm successfully took on the construction of steel roofs, bridges, wrought iron gates, and railings, as well as hot water installations for luxury yachts. In 1886 he was already constructing a number of metal windows, for which there was an increasing demand. In those days each window was individually made. By 1893 the original premises were bursting at the seams and the newly formed Crittall Manufacturing Company Ltd. moved to a new factory at Manor Street. Under its Articles of Association it was empowered to carry on the business of manufacturing windows and casements as well as general engineering. It continued its rapid expansion and by 1905 Crittalls were employing 500 men. In the First World War the factory went over to the production of munitions as well as mountings for machine guns. During this period they were employing 2,000 people, of whom half were women. After the War the mass production techniques used in making shells were adapted to the standardisation of window production. Expansion continued with new factories at neighbouring Witham and Maldon as well as overseas. Among the buildings which installed Crittall windows in the inter-war period were the B.B.C. centre at Portland Place, the Shell-Mex buildings and County Hall, London. During the Second World War the factory again turned to military work and manufactured shells as well as producing ribs for aircraft hangars, equipment for frigates and pontoons, and so on. However, their most vital contribution to the war effort was the construction of Bailey Bridge parts for the Royal Engineers and U.S. Army Engineers. In 1968 the firm was taken over by the Slater Walker Securities Group and subsequently by its present owners, Norcros Ltd. In 1990 the renamed Crittall Windows Ltd. moved to new premises in Springwood Drive and the Manor Road premises were vacated.

In Victorian times the town also supported traditional industries like Youngs Brewery, in Railway Street. Ridleys also had maltings close to the railway station. In 1890 John West & Sons were recorded as being a substantial firm, who from their factory in Sandpit Lane manufactured a wide range of brushes for home, factory and recreational use. Another business contemporary was the Bocking firm of Ashley Adkins & Co. who developed Coir Mat and Matting in a defunct weaving factory, initially using some of the original hand looms.

0. Bocking windmill, *c.*1910, when it was still a working post mill. It subsequently fell into a poor state of repair but in 1994 t was substantially restored to its original appearance. It is the only Grade I listed windmill in Essex.

61. Bocking water-mill, on the River Blackwater, c.1925. Like many watermills it has had a chequered career, having been used in the past for both fulling and flour milling. It is currently unused.

62. These derelict weatherboarded premises in Panfield Lane, seen here in 1926, were where Samuel Courtauld set up his first Silk Mill in 1816. They have since been demolished.

63. Courtauld's Braintree Mill, Chapel Hill, *c*.1915. Courtaulds have now ceased to operate in the town and their factories have been demolished.

64. The former Warner Silk factory at New Mills (left) in South Street, *c*.1910. It was built over 150 years ago by Daniel Walters and later taken over by Warners and Son, who closed the factory in 1971. Part of it has now reopened as a working museum.

65. Sam Watson, an apprentice at work on a hand loom at New Mills in 1901.

66. Hand weaving in remarkably primitive surroundings on one of the old looms at New Mills, *c*.1950.

67. A feature of the work at New Mills was the intricate and beautiful patterns woven on the old machines, *c.*1950. Examples are still made in the working museum.

68. June Swindells working on designs for the wall hangings at Westminster Abbey for the coronation in 1953.

69. An aerial view showing the factory of the Crittall Manufacturing Company Ltd. in Manor Street, *c*.1959.

70. Part of the machine shop at Crittall's, *c*.1935. Power to the individual lathes and other machinery was supplied by way of an overhead belt-driven system.

71 & 72. Crittall's advertising in the 1920s was both novel and eye catching. Models were built on trailers and electric runabouts and went to fêtes, carnivals and exhibitions, with examples of their products.

CRITTALL WINDOWS

FOR THE NEW HOUSES

By specifying STANDARD metal windows—from British Standard 990 : 1945 — you help to reduce the present unavoidable delay in delivery, and at the same time you ensure highest quality and lowest cost. Ask for leaflet 115 B.

THE CRITTALL MANUFACTURING CO. LTD.
BRAINTREE, ENGLAND

73. Ernest Howard Shepard, illustrator of A. A. Milne's *Christopher Robin* and *Winnie the Pooh* books, was employed by Crittall's to advertise their windows.

74. Although the bread and butter work of the company was making standard metal windows, many prestigious jobs were also carried out including these magnificent bronze doors, weighing one and a half tonnes, for the members' entrance to County Hall, London, in 1924. Bronze work was also installed at Selfridges about the same time.

75. W. B. Lake founded his engineering firm in New Street and, on entering a partnership with E. F. Elliot, moved in 1896 into these premises in Rayne Road. At first they specialised in making tools and accessories for the then thriving bicycle trade. Later, they expanded into the manufacture of motor car accessories.

76 & 77. From their early beginnings Lake & Elliot expanded rapidly and in 1905 moved to a new factory at Chapel Hill, which they called the New Albion Works. Here they installed what was reputed to be the first electric furnace in Britain. These two pictures show the iron and steel foundry and the electric furnace, c.1910, crude by present-day standards.

78. At an early date Lake & Elliot were substantial user of electricity, all of which they generated on site. From the same plant they were able to supply electricity to the town and to other local factories. This ceased in 1946 when the mains were connected to the national grid.

79. Lake & Elliot remained a general engineering firm throughout its existence. Here, in the late 1950s, a workman is seen removing the surplus metal from a casting.

80. A general view of the extensive machine shop, *c*.1955.

81. This picture of the mechanised Iron Foundry, *c*.1958, contrasts sharply with the primitive workings in 1910 (see illustrations 76 and 77).

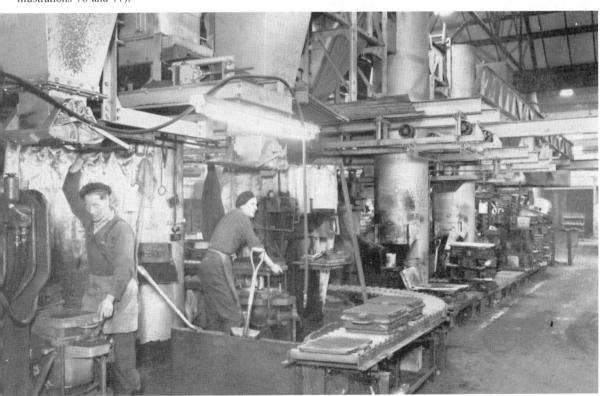

82 & 83. Two examples of the firm's extensive range of jacks.

Chapter 5

Transport

Although built purely for military purposes in connection with their occupation of the country, the intersection of two Roman roads made the site of Braintree a focal point from the time they were built. Later, as the Romans pacified the country, the roads began to be used for trade, leading to some form of settlement at the crossroads. There is also the possibility that the Romans carried supplies along the Blackwater by small barge as was the custom elsewhere in their empire.

Long after the Romans departed, the little town, established by the Bishop of London, became a coaching stage with inns providing overnight accommodation for coaches, private carriages and gigs. Local produce was also brought into the town, either by cart or wagon or on the hoof, for sale in the market. The Chelmsford to Halstead road became a turnpike as did the Braintree to Colchester road, under the control of the Essex Turnpike Trust. Nevertheless, the roads were narrow and muddy and often in very poor condition, so traffic by modern standards was slow and uncomfortable and of limited volume.

Braintree received seaborne trade via Maldon, once the principal port for mid and central Essex; its quays handled outward cargoes of hay, flour, corn and malt, whilst importing timber, coal, salt, lime, slate, oil cake and grain. This was hauled overland along the Maldon—Braintree turnpike, entering the town along the Notley Road. In the 18th century the River Chelmer to Chelmsford was canalised to enable waterborne traffic to pass directly to and from the county town. However, Braintree had to continue to rely on poor roads. Surprisingly, there were no apparent schemes to canalise either the Blackwater or the Brain. However, with the development of the steam locomotive in the early part of the 19th century interest grew in the possibility of Braintree being linked to the coast by means of a railway.

In 1845 plans were deposited with the local Clerk of the Peace for construction of a railway from Braintree through Witham to Maldon, where, as part of the project, it was intended to construct a new dock to cater for the anticipated increase in shipping. In June 1846 Royal Assent was given to an Act of Parliament for the construction of the railway. In addition to stations at Braintree, Witham and Maldon, there were halts at Cressing (at first called Bulford), White Notley as well as others on the Maldon section. Initially, ownership was in the hands of its promoters—the Maldon, Witham and Braintree Railway Company Ltd.—but it was soon purchased by the Eastern Counties Railway, themselves later taken over by the Great Eastern Railway.

The line was built as a double track from Braintree to Maldon and was opened on 2 October 1948; a crowd of several hundred welcomed the first train to arrive in the town. It soon became clear, however, that a single track would suffice and accordingly during the Crimean War one track was lifted and sold to the War Department. Although the line was planned to have a crossing of the main line at Witham, in the end it was constructed as two branches, both running into Witham station. Although started, the planned dock at Maldon was never completed and instead for many years waterborne traffic destined for Witham and Braintree was barged up the Chelmer & Blackwater Navigation to a point where the railway crossed the canal near Maldon, where a special wharf and siding were built to allow the transfer. The new line quickly attracted most of the commercial traffic which had previously used the road and also a considerable amount of new trade. This was facilitated once long distance rail links were established. Of particular importance was the availability for the first time of cheap coal which enabled homes to be kept warm in winter as well as fuelling the new industries which were being established close to the tracks.

Fifteen years after the opening of the railway, the Bishop's Stortford, Dunmow and Braintree Railway was built, connecting the town to the Cambridge main line, which encouraged further traffic. As part of these works a new station was built at Braintree with the original terminus becoming the goods yard. The through connection proved invaluable on at least one occasion during the Second World War, when a bomb blocked the main line at Shenfield so that main line expresses travelling to Ipswich and Norwich were diverted through Braintree, albeit with a speed restriction. In addition, the line was used throughout much of the War for the overnight transportation of bombs destined to be flown from various East Anglian airfields.

The earliest buses in Braintree were operated by Hicks Brothers Ltd. The firm was started in 1878 by Charles and Thomas Hicks in Felsted. Charles was a farmer and Thomas a baker. In 1886 the latter had acquired *The Swan* public house from where he ran a carrier service. By 1914 he was operating a motorised vehicle but the first purpose-built omnibus is thought to have been a 14-seater Ford, purchased in 1914. By 1923 the firm had moved to Fairfield Road; the present garage, now Eastern National property, was built a few years later. Strangely enough, it was built to a style similar to those of the Eastern National garages elsewhere in Essex. A frequent daily service to Chelmsford was started in 1928, where a small bus park in Park Road was established and several other operators were absorbed. By 1949 the company was operating a number of routes fanning out from Braintree, extending to Bishops Stortford and Dunmow in the east, and Colchester, Witham and Rivenhall in the west. In 1950 Hicks Brothers was sold to the British Transport Commission and was finally integrated into the Eastern National in 1955. Another former company operating to Braintree was Moores Brothers Ltd., of Kelvedon. This was also a long-established carrier business whose main service was between Chelmsford and Colchester. However, they also ran buses between Braintree and Colchester as well as from Kelvedon to Braintree. This also was taken over by the Eastern National.

By the beginning of the First World War, the earliest precursor to the present Eastern National—the National Steam Car Company Ltd.—was operating its Clarkson-designed steam-driven buses from its headquarters at Chelmsford to Braintree and Bocking. Eventually the buses were replaced by petrol vehicles which ran in competition with the Hick Bros.' Chelmsford service. Today, the Eastern National Company run most of the services in and around the town, although a smaller and relatively dynamic company, the Hedingham & District Omnibus Company Ltd., has established itself on a number of routes, following its take over in 1960 of the former Letch Bus Service of Sible Hedingham.

84. The Braintree & West Essex Co-operative Society Ltd. held this line-up of road transport in 1914 when most traffic was still horse-drawn.

85. Braintree's first railway station, built in 1849, was the terminus of the line from Maldon and Witham. The buildings comprised a waiting room together with a booking office and storage area. Passengers went through the building to the platform set at right angles. It was replaced in 1869 by the present station. This picture was taken, *c.*1905, when the little building had been taken over as a builder's merchant's office and continued in this use for many years.

EASTERN COUNTIES' RAILWAY.

CHEAP TRIP
TO
LONDON.

On MONDAY, Aug. 13th, 1860,

JOHNSON'S
FIRST SPECIAL
EXCURSION TRAIN,
FOR THE SEASON,

Will leave Braintree Station at 6.30 a.m. calling at Witham at 6.50. a.m., returning from Bishopsgate Station at 8 p.m.

Giving ELEVEN HOURS IN LONDON.

FARES THERE & BACK.

FIRST CLASS.	COVERED CARRIAGES
5s.	2s.6d.

Children, under 12 years of age half-price.

TICKETS may be had up to Saturday, the 11th Inst. of Mr. Finney, Bocking; Mr. Joseph Godfrey Downing, Chemist, Mr. Fred. Andrews, Grocer, and Mr. I. Clayden, Railway Tavern, Braintree; and Railway Stations, Witham and Braintree.

Any further Information may be had of the Contractor

Wm. JOHNSON, Railway Coal Depot.

86. The opening of the railway quickly created a demand by the general public and by 1860 enterprising businessmen had realised the possibilities of cut-price day excursions to London.

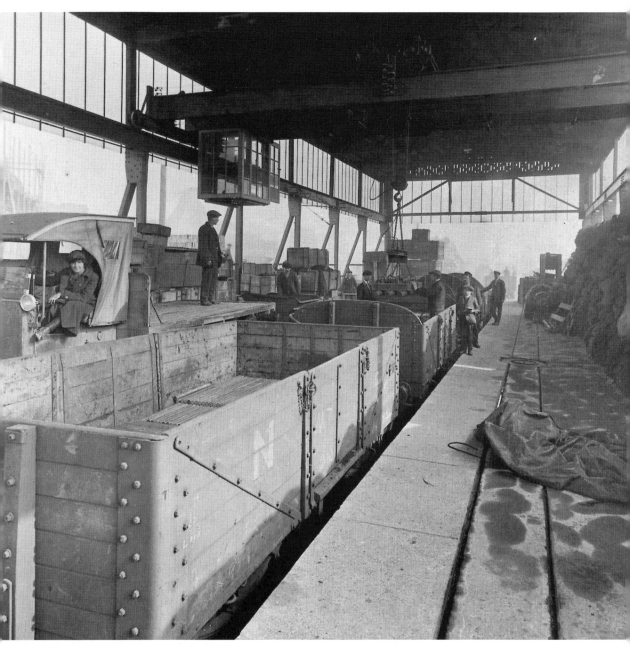

87. Both Crittalls and Lake & Elliot were substantial users of the railway, importing raw materials and consigning their products. Here, at Crittall's Railway Street siding, iron bars are being unloaded from railway waggons, *c.*1915.

88. The exterior of Braintree Station, *c*.1905. This station replaced the original 1848 building when the line was extended to Bishop's Stortford. Although considerably altered, it remains in use and is now the terminus of the branch line.

89. Braintree Railway Station in 1910, looking towards Witham. The double track was only provided at stations to allow trains to pass, otherwise the track was single. The footbridge gave access between the two platforms and was removed in the 1950s. The second track was removed, *c*.1970.

90. A Class F5 steam engine No. 67192 arrives at the station from Witham in April 1949.

91. Steam road vehicles had a brief but important heyday in the final years of the century. Although slow by modern standards, they carried considerable loads. For long distances it was found more convenient for them to be transferred to the railway using specially designed containers—the forerunners of the present road/rail containers.

OSCELYNES
STEAM
EMOVAL SERVICE
LONDON AND ALL PARTS
BRAINTREE
BISHOPS
STORTFORD
JOSCELYNE'S
REMOVAL SERVICE
BRAINTREE
ESSEX

92. The Braintree firm of Joscelynes ran a removal service for many years. At first their vehicles were horse-drawn, then steam (see illustration 91), but with improvements in the reliability of petrol engines they turned to motor lorries but still continued their road/rail operations, *c*.1910.

93. Although Crittall's made extensive use of the railway to transport their products for short hauls, they increasingly made use of motor transport. In this *c*.1920s photograph, metal windows are being delivered locally.

94. The well-known firm of Archer & Sons unusually combined running a soft drink industry with a coal merchant's business. Their first lorry is proudly displayed in the local carnival procession, *c*.1925.

95. Archer & Sons' fleet
of lorries rapidly grew. A
few years later these three
vehicles are seen setting off
from their depot in Manor
Road to deliver soft drinks.

96. This 1930s Commer was
one of a fleet operated by
Joscelynes and proved itself
to be thoroughly reliable.

97. Police Superintendent Lindsay Fulcher in the first Essex police car, a 10/12 HP Belsize saloon outside Braintree Court, with chauffeur, July 1917.

98. In the 1920s and '30s bus and coach companies sprung up. One was Horn Coaches, who ran a fast coach route to London from Braintree Bus Park following closely the old 18th- and 19th-century coaching route to London. Their garage was at the rear of the *Horn Hotel*. They were taken over by the Eastern National in 1935.

99. The former Essex bus and coach company, Hicks Bros. Ltd., was founded at the turn of the century, running buses from Felsted to Braintree, to where it moved in 1922. Early vehicles included Ford T trucks with bolt-on chassis, a Daimler, an Austin 20 and an Armstrong Siddeley. Mr. E. Hicks is a passenger in this bus, c.1906 (extreme right). The driver is Mr. W. Ardley and the conductor Mr. L. Woodley.

100. Another local bus company which operated in the 1920s was Hutley's, who ran a service between Braintree and Colchester. Mr. A. Hutley himself is standing proudly beside the driver's seat. The conductor Mr. E. Brown, dressed in the customary white overcoat, is standing on the freeboard.

101. This Leyland Lion bus was one of the early service buses operated by Hicks Bros. Ltd. The logo was handwritten on all their buses from the late 1920s until the limited liability company was formed in May 1935. It was replaced by the rising sun motif.

102. A Hicks Bros. 1930s single-decker Leyland bus at Braintree Bus Park. Despite the proximity of their own garage, the company made extensive use of the park which it shared with other operators.

103. This smart 1930s coach stands at the entrance to Hicks Bros. garage in Fairfield Road, ready for an outing, possibly the seaside, an ever popular destination during the summer months.

104. Letch's Motor Services was one of the older bus companies operating in and around Braintree. It were founded in 1919 by Aubrey Letch at Sible Hedingham. He built up a series of routes between Braintree, Halstead and Sudbury, using a rather miscellaneous collection of vehicles including this secondhand Crossley DD42/5, which was new to Plymouth City Transport in 1947.

HICKS BROS., Ltd.

REVISED WEEKLY TICKET RATES
commencing Monday, 24th February, 1936.

BRAINTREE–CHELMSFORD ROUTE No. 11.

		6-Day.	5-Day.
Little Waltham to Chelmsford	*Adult*	**3/-**	**2/6**
„ „ „ „	*Child*	**1/6**	**1/6**
Broomfield Green to Chelmsford	*Adult*	**1/9**	**1/6**
„ „ „ „	*Child*	**1/3**	**1/-**
Broomfield Post Office to Chelmsford	*Adult*	**1/6**	**1/3**
„ „ „ „ „	*Child*	**1/-**	**10d.**

Other Weekly Tickets as usual. Children Half Fare.

DUNMOW–CHELMSFORD ROUTE No. 21.

		6-Day.	5-Day.
Howe Street to Chelmsford	*Adult*	**3/6**	**3/-**
„ „ „ „	*Child*	**2/-**	**1/9**
Great Waltham to Chelmsford	*Adult*	**3/-**	**2/6**
„ „ „ „	*Child*	**1/9**	**1/6**
Broomfield Green to Chelmsford	*Adult*	**1/9**	**1/6**
„ „ „ „	*Child*	**1/3**	**1/-**
Broomfield Post Office to Chelmsford	*Adult*	**1/6**	**1/3**
„ „ „ „ „	*Child*	**1/-**	**10d.**

Other Weekly Tickets as usual, Children Half Fare.

The Shearcroft Printing Co., Ltd., Market Place, Braintree.

105. This leaflet issued by Hicks Bros. Ltd. on 24 February 1936 provides details of the fares on what was always their most frequent and profitable routes—the Dunmow and Braintree routes to Chelmsford.

106. Passengers wait patiently for the driver to arrive so that the Moores Colchester service can depart from Braintree Bus Park, *c*.1950. Behind is a glimpse of Sams Bus Park Café, once an important meeting place for travellers.

107. Two double deckers line up at Braintree Bus Park, *c*.1955. On the left a former Hicks Bros. bus has been repainted in Eastern National colours following its takeover on 1 January 1950. On the right is an Eastern National bus. Their No. 23 service was their only local route until the acquisition of Hicks Bros. Ltd.

Chapter 6

Public Services

Local Government

The former Braintree Urban District Council was set up towards the end of the last century and took over the responsibilities of the earlier Local Board of Health, as well as various other duties. However, this area excluded the parish of Bocking, which was administered as part of the Braintree Rural District, and it was not until 1934 that the parish was transferred into a united district with Braintree, in belated recognition that the two communities had physically merged into one town. In 1928 Sir W. J. Courtauld presented the town with the impressive two-storeyed neo-Georgian Town Hall, built next to the Market Square. For many years it provided a home for the entire council staff as well as housing an ornate Council Chamber and Committee Rooms. However, in 1974 there were major changes to local government and the new greatly enlarged Braintree District Council was formed. This resulted in a search for new accommodation, which has now been provided in Bocking End. The former Town Hall is used as a Tourist Centre.

Hospitals

There are two National Health Service hospitals in Braintree. The present William Julien Courtauld Hospital in London Road was built and presented to the town in 1921 by Sir William, as a replacement for an earlier cottage hospital in Broad Road (founded by Sydney Courtauld in 1871). Initially, the new hospital had 28 beds. It was enlarged in 1938, together with an 11-bed maternity unit, following a public subscription, and endowed by Sir William. In 1948 it was taken over by the National Health Service, which was created by the post-war Labour Government to replace voluntary health care, at the time generally considered to be outmoded and inadequate for the nation's needs. William Julien Courtauld Hospital currently deals with general care and maternity. St Michael's Hospital, in Rayne Road, dating back to 1837, was built as a workhouse on a three-acre site by the Braintree Union to accommodate some 300 people. Here, in Victorian times inmates were expected to work from six in the morning to six at night. It was later taken over by the Essex County Council when they assumed a statutory public assistance role. Currently, it specialises in dealing with older people. Today, both hospitals are part of the Mid Essex Hospital Trust, based at Broomfield near Chelmsford and the future of St Michael's is in some doubt.

Education

In Victorian times the Churches played an important role in the provision of elementary education. The Church of England founded National Schools, whilst the Nonconformists ran British Schools. Later, the local authority began to play an increasingly dominant role in the provision of education. Great emphasis was placed on the 'three R's'—Reading, (W)riting and (A)rithmetic. Strong classroom discipline meant that standards in these early elementary schools were surprisingly high, even if the classes were large, and buildings primitive and cramped with little or no equipment. The Education Act of 1944 brought sweeping changes, existing elementary schools became primary schools and senior schools became secondary schools. School leaving age was raised by stages to 16, so that all children and not just the fortunate few received secondary education. By 1950 there were three primary schools in the town: Manor Street Junior and Infants, Bocking County Primary, Bocking End and Braintree Church of England in New Street. Secondary Education was provided by Braintree County High, opened in 1907, and Braintree Secondary Modern (later the Margaret Tabor High School). Today, keeping pace with a growing population, a number of additional primary and secondary schools have been built within the town, whilst some of the older buildings have been replaced or rebuilt. One of these includes the old Manor Road School which in 1993 opened as Braintree's principal museum.

Police Force

The Essex County Police Force was established in 1840, its headquarters being at Old Court, Springfield, Chelmsford, with a total force of 138 men for the whole of the county. Braintree came within the Hinckford area, with a total of 19 officers. By 1888 the Hinckford Division was employing 35 officers, of whom nine were stationed at Braintree and one at Bocking. The first police station was built in Rayne Road, four years after the county force was set up. It was replaced in 1872 by a new station in Fairfield Road built by the same contractor as the much larger Romford Station. Although becoming increasingly crowded, the station remained in use until 1993 when it was replaced by new premises in The Avenue, built at a cost of £2 million.

Fire Brigade

As separate authorities, Braintree and Bocking each ran their own fire brigades until the two bodies merged in 1934. Initially, the appliances were quite primitive, being small carts with a hand pump, but eventually they became more sophisticated. A further step forward took place when at the beginning of the Second World War all local fire brigades were merged into a National Fire Service. After the War the responsibility for fire fighting returned to local authorities and today it is the duty of the Essex County Fire and Rescue Service. For many years they maintained a small fire station in Swan Lane, but new premises have now been provided in Railway Street.

Gasworks

The town's first gasworks was built in New Street about 1840 but was superseded by another in Manor Street, which had the advantage of easy access to coal delivered to the railway goods yard. Here, considerable expansion of the Braintree and Bocking Gas Company Ltd. took place. Mains were laid under most of the roads in the built-up area and gas became widely used for lighting, cooking and heating. Before the establishment of the Gasworks, some streets in the town were illuminated at night by oil lamps which were replaced by gas until, in turn, electricity came. Gas was nationalised by the post-war Labour Government but continued to be made at Braintree until the early 1950s, when a high pressure main was laid from Witham. Here, it was linked to a similar main running between newly modernised works at Chelmsford and Colchester—the beginnings of a gas grid. Today, British Gas and other firms supply the town with natural North Sea Gas via a national gas grid and the environmentally polluting method of producing gas from coal has ceased. The old gasworks is now merely a distribution centre.

Electricity

The adoption of electricity for lighting and power was slower to develop than gas. From about the turn of the century there were a few commercial undertakings and a small number of large houses had their own private generators. However, in 1917 Lake & Elliot built their own power house to generate electricity for their own requirements. They were also able to supply neighbouring firms and the town itself. In 1946 the mains were connected to the national electricity grid and Lake & Elliot ceased to operate their own generator. However, many outlying houses were not connected to the supply until the late 1940s when the newly created state-owned Eastern Electricity Board erected power lines to all properties as part of the Labour Government's crash programme to supply electricity to every property throughout the country. In the 1990s electricity generation and supply was returned to the private sector.

Water and Sewerage

Water supplies and sewerage arrangements were developed over a long period by local authorities. Before 1888 responsibility lay with the two Local Boards of Health. In 1864 a waterworks was established in Notley Road, next to the River Brain. Earlier, water came from the Town Pump in New Street and shallow wells. Later, the water was obtained by artesian wells. Sewerage often ran from crude cesspools into open ditches, causing pollution and ill health and sometimes even death. Preventing the spread of cholera was a particular problem. After 1888, the former Urban District Council provided water from their works to the area south of the old A120 (Rayne Road/Coggeshall Road) whilst the former Braintree Rural District Council provided water to the north. Both had their own boreholes, though by 1950 the two sets of mains had become linked. Sewage disposal for Braintree and Bocking had a similar arrangement, with the sewers flowing by gravity to their own works. Today, both water supply and sewerage disposal are under unified control and are the responsibility of the Anglian Water Company Ltd., with the sewage works sited next to the new bypass.

108. Braintree Town Hall, *c.*1935. This impressive neo-Georgian building was presented to the town by Sir W. J. Courtauld in 1928 and was the heart of local administration for over 40 years. It is now a tourist centre. As a result of local authority changes in 1974 new council premises have been built in Bocking End.

109. An artist's impression of the ornate council chamber as it appeared in 1928. The panelling and much of the furniture was made from English oak.

110. In 1933 a post office was built in Fairfield Road. Like so many others of the era its design was neo-Georgian which fortuitously matched that of the adjacent Town Hall. Standing on the steps are G. Thorpe Bartram J.P., O.B.E., Chairman of the Council, together with two post office employees, Miss J. E. Rush, who issued the first stamp and Mr. Ch. Rich who issued the first postal order. Previously the post office was at 60 High Street. In 1994 it moved into the 'Quadrant'.

111. The police station, c.1900, was another public building in Fairfield Road and has now been replaced. It was built in 1872 superseding the town's first station in Rayne Road.

112. At the same time as the police station was built, accommodation for the officers was being provided. The attractive railings seen here were removed for the war effort. The photograph was taken in *c*.1900.

113. As separate authorities Braintree and Bocking each ran their own fire brigades until they merged in 1934. A first both brigades had simpl handcarts, as can be seen in the illustration below which shows the Braintree team, *c*.1892.

BRAINTREE LOCAL BOARD

1887

114. The brigade handcarts were gradually phased out to make way for the motor vehicle, and here Superintendent H. Lawrence of the Bocking brigade poses with his new motor vehicle and seated crew, *c*.1924. All the firemen were part-timers.

115. The Braintree & Bocking Institute—now called simply 'The Institute'—as it appeared *c*.1905. It was founded as the Literary and Mechanics' Institution in 1845 but was rebuilt at a cost of £3,000 in 1863 following a bequest from George Courtauld. Over the years it has been used for a wide range of town activities from theatre groups to dog shows.

116. In 1878 the Salvation Army was founded in the East End of London. Within a few years there were followers all over the country. This group picture was taken in 1922 at the Salvation Army Hall, Rayne Road. Seated in the centre is Bandmaster French and his wife, with Captain A. Sharp on his right.

117. St Michael's Hospital, *c.*1905, then the Braintree Union Workhouse. The building has since been substantially altered both internally and externally. It is now within the National Health Service and deals with the elderly.

Education

18. The interior of Manor Street School, *c.*1905. The school was built in 1863 to a design fairly typical of the times. The infants' class and its teachers have been carefully positioned in one part of the large room. Today, much of the fabric remains unchanged although it is now a museum.

19. Children from Manor Street School, Braintree, pose for their group photograph, August 1908.

120. Bocking School, Church Street, and Group 11 pose with their teachers. Despite the comparative poverty of the times, children were usually clean and neatly dressed. Strong parental and classroom discipline often led to excellent scholastic results.

121. Bocking School, Church Street, c.1921, and the football team with their linesman and master.

122. The County High School, Coggeshall Road, *c*.1925, was built by the Essex County Council in 1907 on land given by Mrs. Sydney Courtauld, of Bocking Place. One of the first governors was Sir W. J. Courtauld J.P. It has now been replaced by the Tabors High School.

123. In 1922, Bocking Place became the Braintree Intermediate School. It was the first of its kind in Essex. Its aim was to provide a level of education between that of local senior schools and grammar schools but was incorporated into the High School in 1938. Here, across the extensive grounds, *c*.1925, the school buildings can be glimpsed.

124. Photographed in his study, *c.*1925, Mr. G. A. Birnage B.Sc. was the headmaster of Braintree Intermediate School for the whole of its existence.

125. The science room at Braintree Intermediate School, *c.*1925. The equipment appears to be rather meagre but the class is small, unlike many in today's schools.

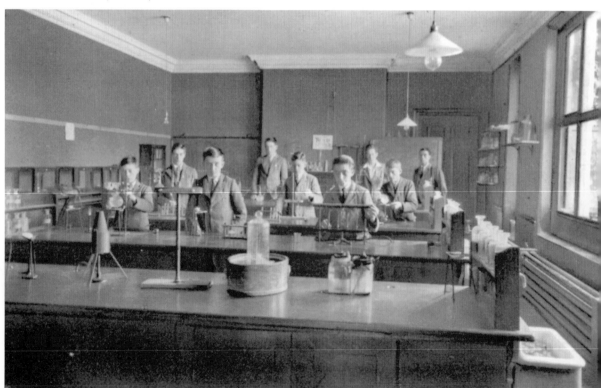

Chapter 7

Wartime

Braintree and Bocking played their full part in both World Wars. Most able-bodied men were called up for military service, many in the Essex Regiment or the Essex Yeomanry, and fought with distinction in the different theatres of war. On the home front the factories were mostly engaged in war production, with the engineering firms producing armaments.

In the First World War numbers of soldiers were stationed in and around the town, being part of the strategic reserve held against surprise invasion by the enemy. Although air attack was in its infancy, the town suffered several raids by Zeppelins.

During the Second World War the town was more directly involved. Although not a major enemy target, nevertheless throughout the war some 6,378 bombs were dropped on the town and eight lives were lost with many more injured. The worst occasion was a night raid on 16 February 1941 when a substantial part of the centre of the town was badly damaged. Lloyds Bank received a direct hit. Another bomb fell opposite Braintree High School smashing its front, and most of the windows in Bank Street and some in High Street were shattered. Sadly, three people were killed and 17 injured in this particular engagement. The town was also attacked by Doodlebugs (V1s or flying bombs) when one fell in Notley Road, close to Notley Place, causing a massive explosion and a blast which was felt in the Market Square. In 1944, Hitler's second secret weapon, the V2 rocket, began to fall haphazardly throughout the area, without any warning by day and night. Fortunately the majority fell harmlessly in fields and woods and caused no damage in the town itself.

In 1940, after the fall of France, Britain was threatened with invasion and various measures were taken to help in the country's defence. A citizens' army was quickly created, throughout the country, mainly recruited from men too old or young to be of military service. At first the force was known as the Local Defence Volunteers, but Churchill quickly changed the name to the Home Guard. Initially they were armed with home-made weapons like pikes, made from butchers' knives fixed to the end of broomsticks, but as the war progressed they became more suitably equipped with rifles and other arms. The Braintree Home Guard, numbering some 200 men, met at the Drill Hall and there was also a Signals Company based at the Fairfield Road Post Office.

With the entry of the United States of America into the war, Essex and East Anglia generally became the host to a large number of military airfields which were hurriedly constructed for use by the 8th U.S. Army Air Force in their joint campaign with the R.A.F. against the enemy.

Several of these airfields, like Wethersfield, Rivenhall, Gosfield and Boreham were constructed within a few miles of the town. Consequently, during the latter part of the Second World War the town was much frequented by off-duty airmen looking for an opportunity to escape for a short time from military discipline, hardship and war dangers.

It was during this period that a Military Hospital was built in the grounds of White Court, previously a large detached house standing in its own grounds in London Road. It consisted largely of Nissen huts linked to one another by sheltered walkways. Initially, it had 750 beds, later increased to 834. Following D-Day, 6 June 1944, it was further expanded by the erection of tented wards. To begin with, many of those treated were injured and sick U.S. airmen from local airfields, but following the invasion of Europe by the Allies specially equipped hospital trains, loaded with injured soldiers, began to arrive at Braintree railway station from the battlefields. A total of 13 such trains were eventually received. On 19 April 1944 the hospital was the subject of an air attack, when an enemy raider dropped several bombs on the complex, possibly intended for a large supply dump nearby. Many of the wards were damaged but luckily no one was killed or seriously injured. The hospital was closed by 13 June 1945 and for some years lay derelict. More recently the site has been redeveloped for housing.

Braintree celebrated V.E. Day 1945 with a massive street party in the Market Place. The Town Hall and the central fountain were illuminated for the first time since the beginning of the war and several thousand people, including Allied and British servicemen, danced outside to music relayed from the Town Hall, which was decorated with flags of all the Allies. Celebrations continued until the early hours. Public houses received special permission to remain open until midnight. The substantial American presence in and around the town was not forgotten in the celebrations and symbolically Major Alice Howard, of the American Army Hospital, officially hoisted the victory flag over the parish church.

126. During the First World War substantial numbers of soldiers were stationed in and around the town as part of a strategic reserve held against any surprise invasion by the enemy. Many families had soldiers billeted on them. In this picture, Harry Hicks stands with his wife and family, outside his shop in Bocking Church Street, together with men from the Notts. and Derby Regiment.

127 & 128. During both the First and Second World Wars the main factories in the town turned to war work. At Crittall's, with the men away in the forces, women were employed to make artillery shells and achieved very high productivity levels.

129. Before the First World War the government only employed specialist firms on munition work. In the early part of the war a severe shortage of armaments resulted in heavy British casualties. To rectify this, engineering firms such as Crittalls were contracted to mass produce shells. Seen here, *c*.1916, are workmen engaged in making fuses.

130-131. This attractive plaster and timber-framed house was formerly the Manse to the Coggeshall Road Baptist church. It was destroyed in an air raid together with the adjacent Braintree Motor garage (below). The site is now part of Sainsbury's car park.

132. On 16 February 1941, Braintree suffered a night raid when several bombs were dropped on the town. One fell in Bank Street destroying Lloyds Bank and adjacent shops. This picture was taken after the debris was removed. Redevelopment took place after the war, but the new buildings were set back permitting the road to be widened. Like so much new development, they were not of a style in keeping with the traditional appearance of the town.

R.B.1
16
SERIAL NO.
1

MINISTRY OF FOOD

M of F

AK 341142

1953-1954

RATION BOOK

Surname .... SUCKLING .... Initials ... CHARLOTTE

Address ...... 30 Manor St

Braintree

Essex

IF FOUND RETURN TO ANY FOOD OFFICE		F.O. CODE No.
		E -- C 3

133. During both the world wars supplies to Britain were badly disrupted and as a result food and clothing rationing was quickly introduced. At the beginning of the Second World War each person received a ration book containing sets of 'coupons', given up each week in exchange for a set quantity of supplies. Rationing continued for some years after the war ended.

PURE DRIED WHOLE EGGS U.S.A.

THIS PACKAGE MUST BE KEPT **IN A COOL DRY PLACE** AWAY FROM ANYTHING HAVING A STRONG SMELL.

THIS PACKAGE CONTAINS **12 EGGS** IN POWDER FORM

5 OUNCES NET WEIGHT EQUAL TO 12 EGGS

TO OPEN
CUT OFF SEALED END OF INNER BAG.
AFTER USE, REFOLD BAG TO PROTECT CONTENTS.

Pure dried whole eggs in powder form
Issued by Ministry of Food

DIRECTIONS FOR USING

One level tablespoon dried egg with two table-spoons water equals one egg.

Put the dried egg into a clean bowl, add the water and mix until smooth. Work out lumps with a spoon against the side of the bowl. Whip slightly with a fork or whisk.

Suitable for making scrambled eggs, ome-lets and for use in all cooked recipes which normally require fresh eggs. This egg when mixed will keep only as long as fresh beaten egg.

PRICE 1s. 9d.

134. There were shortages of fresh eggs throughout the Second World War and for much of the time the housewife used cartons of dried egg powder. It was reconstituted by adding water and made reasonable omelettes, egg dishes and cakes. It proved remarkably popular and even now is remembered with some affection.

135. The war resulted in the closure of many small businesses. In the Soft Drink Industry supplies were 'pooled' and produced at a limited number of depots. Among the casualties was the long established Archer & Sons, which was taken over by James MacPherson of Cottage Place, Chelmsford, where all local manufacturing was concentrated. Britvic, also of Chelmsford, eventually took MacPherson's over.

MANUFACTURERS AND DISTRIBUTING AGENTS.

C. R. ARCHER

TELEPHONE:
BRAINTREE 36.

Works :
80, MANOR STREET, BRAINTREE.

MANOR STREET,
BRAINTREE,

12th January, 1943.

DEAR SIR or MADAM,

Due to War-time conditions, and circumstances beyond our control, we have decided to relinquish the manufacture of Mineral Waters in this district.

We are sincerely grateful for the excellent support you have given us over a number of years, and assure you that it is in your interests that we have come to this decision. You are aware of the introduction of the Government's scheme of concentration of the Soft Drinks Industry shortly to operate, and we had no alternative but to entrust your future supplies to the competent hands of Messrs. James, Macpherson & Co., Ltd., of Chelmsford, who, we feel sure, will endeavour to meet your future requirements.

Yours faithfully,

per pro Archer & Sons,

Charles Robert Archer.

136. White Court, London Road, was originally known as Oaklands. During the war it became the home to a large military hospital and linked Nissen huts were built in the grounds. Here, many injured U.S. airmen were treated and later many battlefield casualties arrived via Braintree Railway Station in special hospital trains.

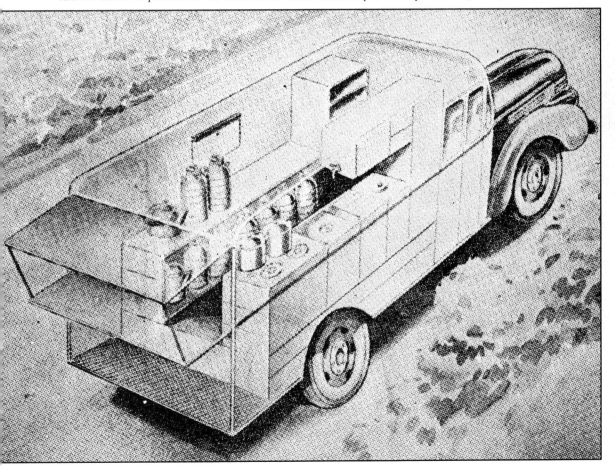

THE BRAINTREE SAVINGS BANK 53-599

No. 1913 Y

SOUTH BRAINTREE, MASS November 22 1940

PAY TO THE
ORDER OF British War Relief Society, Inc. $2,000 00

DOLLARS

TO THE FIRST NATIONAL BANK OF BOSTON 5-39
BOSTON, MASS.

One Rolling Kitchen for Braintree, England

TREASURER

137. Throughout the Second World War Braintree, Massachusetts, provided the town with welfare assistance by sending food parcels and also provided funds for three mobile kitchens.

138. An artist's impression of one of the three mobile kitchens provided by Braintree, Massachusetts.

139. A group picture of 'E' Company, 11th Essex Battalion, Home Guard, formed to protect the Home Front from German invasion. They met at the Drill Hall in Victoria Street, normally the base of the local Territorial unit.

Recreation

140. Braintree Open Air Swimming Baths were opened in 1914 and closed in the late 1960s. Here, Miss Belle White, British Olympic Champion, takes the high board in the first ever swimming gala. In comparison with today's heated indoor pools, they offered very spartan facilities and the limited depth under the diving board would now be considered dangerous. In summer the baths were popular for family outings and many enthusiasts would turn up whatever the weather.

141. Well before the days of purpose-built pools, bathers swam in any suitable stretch of water. Mill pools were often used and crude diving boards and huts installed. Here, members of the Braintree & Bocking Swimming Club pose in front of their changing hut next to the River Blackwater at Bocking in 1908.

142. Football is an ever popular sport and most of the local firms had their own teams, with strong rivalry between them. Here, the 1923-4 Courtauld United Football Junior Team proudly display their hard won trophy outside the pavilion.

FOOTBALL FIXTURES - SEASON 1924-25.

CRITTALLS' 1ST XI.

Date	Opponents	Comp.	Gr'nd
Aug. 30			
Sept. 6	Halstead	B H C C	H
13			
20	Maldon Town	N E L	H
27			
Oct. 4	Burnham Ramblers	N E L	H
11		E J C	
18	Courtauld's United	N E L	H
25	Heybridge	N E L	H
		E J C	
Nov. 1			
8	Courtauld's United	N E L	A
15	R.F.A.	E & S B L	H
22			
29	Halstead	N E L	H
Dec. 6	Springfield	N E L	A
13	Mildmay's	N E L	H
20			
25			
B.D. 26			
27	Heybridge	E & S B L	H
1925			
Jan. 3	Maldon St. Mary's	N E L	A
10	Halstead	E & S B L	A
17	Maldon Town	N E L	A
24			
31	Heybridge	E & S B L	A
Feb. 7	Maldon Town	E & S B L	H
14	Crompton's	N E L	A
21	R.F.A.	E & S B L	A
28	Heybridge	N E L	A
Mar. 7			
14			
21	Maldon St. Mary's	N E L	H
28	Maldon Town	E & S B L	A
April 4	Crompton's	N E L	H
11	Mildmay's	N E L	A
E.M. 13			
18			
25	Burnham Ramblers	N E L	A
May 2			

LAKE & ELLIOT'S 1ST XI.

Date	Opponents	Comp.	Gr'nd
Aug. 30	Practice Match		H
Sept. 6	Halstead Factory Sports Club	H & D L	H
13	Courtaulds' United Reserves	N E L	A
		E J C	
20			
27	Great Yeldham United	H & D L	H
Oct. 4		E J C	
11			
18	Great Yeldham United	H & D L	A
25	Witham Town	B & D L	H
Nov. 1	Springfield	N E L	A
8	Rayne	N E L	H
15	Felstead Rovers	B & D L	A
22	Courtaulds' United Reserves	N E L	A
29	Rayne	B & D L	A
Dec. 6	Springfield	N E L	H
13	Witham Town	B & D L	A
20	Rayne	B & D L	A
B.D. 26	Earls Colne	H & D L	H
27	Halstead Reserves	H & D L	H
Jan. 3	Crittalls' Reserves	N E L	A
10	Rayne	N E L	A
17	Felstead Rovers	B & D L	H
31	Witham Town	N E L	H
Feb. 7	Maldon St. Mary's Reserves	N E L	A
14	Crittalls' Reserves	N E L	H
21	Witham Town	N E L	A
28	Crittalls' Reserves	B & D L	H
Mar. 7	Maldon St Mary's Reserves	N E L	A
14	Crittalls' Reserves	B & D L	A
28	Halstead Reserves	H & D L	A
April 11	Halstead Factory Sports Club	H & D L	A
E.M. 13	Earls Colne	H & D L	A

COURTAULDS' 1ST XI.

Date	Opponents	Comp.	Gr'nd
Sept. 6	Mildmay Athletic	N E L	A
		E J C	
27	Cromptons' Athletic	N E L	H
		E J C	
Oct. 18	Crittalls	N E L	A
25	Maldon Town	N E L	A
Nov. 8	Crittalls	N E L	H
15	Cambridge A.	H & D L	A
22	Maldon St. Mary's	N E L	H
Dec. 6	Heybridge	N E L	A
13	Maldon Town	N E L	H
20	Saffron Walden	H & D L	A
Jan. 3	Halstead Town	N E L	H
10	Cromptons' Athletic	N E L	A
24	Halstead Town	N E L	A
31	Haverhill Rovers	H & D L	A
Feb. 7	Heybridge	N E L	H
21	Haverhill Rovers	H & D L	H
28	Cambridge A.	H & D L	H
Mar. 7	Burnham Ramblers	N E L	A
14	Saffron Walden	H & D L	A
21	Mildmay Athletic	N E L	H
April 4	Maldon St. Mary's	N E L	A
25	Burnham Ramblers	N E L	H

CRITTALLS' 2ND XI.

Date	Opponents	Comp.	Gr'nd
Aug. 30			
Sept. 6	Felstead	B & D L	A
Oct. 11	Rayne	B & D L	H
18	Courtauld's United R.	N E L	A
Nov. 8	Courtauld's United R.	N E L	H
15	Witham	B & D L	A
29	Witham	N E L	A
Dec. 6	Witham	B & D L	H
13	Maldon St. Mary's R.	N E L	A
27	Rayne	B & D L	A
1925			
Jan. 3	Lake & Elliot	N E L	H
17	Rayne	N E L	H
24	Maldon St. Mary's R.	N E L	H
Feb. 14	Lake & Elliot	N E L	A
21	Rayne	N E L	A
28	Lake & Elliot	B & D L	A
Mar. 7	Springfield	N E L	A
14	Lake & Elliot	B & D L	H
28	Springfield	N E L	H
April 4			H
11	Felstead	B & D L	H
E.M. 13			H
May 2	Witham	N E L	H

LAKE & ELLIOTS' 2ND XI.

Date	Opponents	Comp.	Gr'nd
Aug. 30	Coggeshall Reserves	Fr'ndly	H
Sept. 6	Bocking St. Peter's	Fr'ndly	H
13	Chappel	K L	A
20	Warren Old Boys	B & D L	H
27	Coggeshall Athletic	B & D L	A
Oct. 4	Y. M. C. A.	B & D L	A
11	Copford United	K L	H
18	Bocking St. Peter's	B & D L	H
25	Felstead Reserves	Fr'ndly	A
Nov. 1	Langford	Fr'ndly	H
8	Intermediate Old Boys	B & D L	A
15	Tiptree Heath	K L	H
22	Warren Old Boys	B & D L	A
29	Coggeshall Athletic	B & D L	H
Dec. 6	Bocking St. Peter's	B & D L	A
13	Intermediate Old Boys	B & D L	H
20	Courtaulds' Juniors	B & D L	A
27	Y. M. C. A.	K L	A
1925			
Jan. 3	Earls Colne Rovers	K L	A
10	Courtaulds' Juniors	B & D L	H
17	Wickham Bishops	K L	A
24	Y. M. C. A.	B & D L	H
31	Langford	Fr'ndly	A
Feb. 7	Crittalls' Juniors	B & D L	H
14	Copford United	K L	A
21	Chappel	K L	H
Mar. 7	Feering	K L	A
14	Tiptree Heath	K L	H
28	Crittalls' Juniors	B & D L	H
April 4	Feering	K L	H
11	Wickham Bishops	K L	H
E.M. 13	Y. M. C. A. (10.30 a.m.)	K L	H
25	Earls Colne Rovers	K L	H

COURTAULDS' 2ND XI.

Date	Opponents	Comp.	Gr'nd
Sept. 13	Lake & Elliots	N E L	H
Oct. 11	Witham	N E L	H
18	Crittalls' Reserves	N E L	H
Nov. 1	Halstead Factory	B & D L	A
8	Crittall's Reserves	N E L	A
15	Earls Colne	B & D L	H
22	Lake & Elliots	N E L	A
29	Halstead Town Res.	B & D L	H
Dec. 6	Maldon St. Mary's R.	N E L	H
13	Coggeshall	B & D L	A
27	Rayne	N E L	A
1925			
Jan. 3	Halstead Factory	B & D L	A
10	Halstead Town Res.	B & D L	H
17	Witham	N E L	A
24	Rayne	N E L	H
Feb. 14	Kelvedon	B & D L	H
21	Earls Colne	B & D L	A
Mar. 7	Coggeshall	B & D L	H
14	Kelvedon	B & D L	A
April 11	Springfield	N E L	H
18	Maldon St. Mary's R.	N E L	A
25	Springfield	N E L	A

B H C C—Braintree Hospital Charity Cup. N E L—North Essex League. E J C—Essex Junior Cup. E & S B L—Essex & Suffolk Border League.
B & D L—Braintree & District League. H & D L—Haverhill & District League. K L—Kelvedon League. H—Home. A—Away.

143. Various teams competed in the unsponsored leagues. This extract from a 1924 town guide gives details of the season's fixtures for the three main works teams.

144. Before television, most people visited the movies at least once a week. For many years Braintree had two cinemas, The Central and The Palace (later The Embassy). The Central was in High Street, on a site now occupied by Townrows departmental stores. Here, *c*.1928, the film idol Rudolph Valentino stars in the hit of the year, 'The Eagle'.

★ SHIPMAN & KING CINEMAS ★

EMBASSY MALDON
PHONE 168

SUN., DEC. 20, 4.30-10 p.m. : Robert Mitchum, HOLIDAY AFFAIR ⓒ
Roddy McDowall, KILLER SHARK ⓒ

THURS., DEC. 17th	MON., DEC. 21st
Cecil Eileen Donald PARKER ★ HERLIE ★ WOLFIT *Isn't Life Wonderful* (Tech.) 3.15. 6.10, 9.10. ⓒ GEORGE BRENT **TANGIER INCIDENT** 1.45. 4.40, 7.35. ⓐ	**The Greatest Warrior** of them all ! **HIAWATHA** (Colour). 3.10, 6.5, 9.5. ⓒ THE BOWERY BOYS **JALOPY** 2 p.m., 4.55, 7.50. ⓤ

EMBASSY BRAINTREE
PHONE 78

SUN.. DEC. 20, 4.30-10 p.m. : John Wayne, DARK COMMAND ⓐ
Robert Lowery, ARSON INC. ⓐ

THURS., DEC. 17th	MON., DEC. 21st, for 5 Days.
GARY COOPER *Return to Paradise* (Tech.) 1.50, 5.10, 8.35. ⓐ JOHN PAYNE COLEEN GRAY *The Secret Four* 3.20, 6.40. ⓐ	CLOSED XMAS DAY. RICHARD TODD ★ GLYNIS JOHNS in Walt Disney's *The Sword and The Rose* (Tech.) 2.30, 5.30, 8.30. ⓤ Walt Disney's WATER BIRDS 1.15, 4.10, 7.10. ⓤ

CENTRAL BRAINTREE
PHONE 78

THURS., DEC. 17th	MON., DEC. 21st
RICHARD TODD JOAN RICE in *Walt Disney's* **THE STORY OF ROBIN HOOD** AND HIS MERRIE MEN (Tech.) 5.50, 8.45. Sat. 3 p.m. ⓤ Tim Holt: **Storm Over Wyoming** 4.45, 7.40. Sat. 1.55. ⓤ	JOHNNY SHEFFIELD **BOMBA** & THE AFRICAN TREASURE 6.10, 9 p.m. ⓤ ALEC GUINESS ★ KAY WALSH **LAST HOLIDAY** 4.35, 7.25. ⓤ

CHILDREN'S MATINEE EVERY SATURDAY.   6d., 9d., 1/-.

145. In later years both The Central and the more modern Embassy were in common ownership. Their programmes for the period beginning 17 December 1953 are listed here.

146. The entrance to the public gardens, *c*.1910. Encompassing 5½ acres, the gardens were once part of the grounds of Mrs. George Courtauld's house. When opened in 1888 they were still surrounded by farmland. Today, with the expanding built up area, they are perhaps of even greater amenity value than in the last century.

147. The ornamental water feature in the public gardens as it appeared in *c*.1905.

Events

148. King George V's Silver Jubilee was celebrated in festive style by these employees of Courtaulds, who were appropriately dressed in sailor suits standing in front a model of an ocean liner.

149. The High Street on Market Day, about the turn of the century. Goods and animals were then sold in the road and farmers and traders would gather outside the Corn Exchange and the *Horn Hotel*, an old coaching inn.

150. Employees of the Braintree and West Essex Co-operative Society Ltd. set out from the Central Stores at Bocking End on their annual outing to Clacton, *c*.1885.

151. The local hunt meet at the *White Hart Hotel*, Braintree, *c*.1905.

152. At the annual May Fair, *c*.1905, one of the big attractions was Chas Thurston with his impressive bioscope. Attracting fairgoers to the 6.30 p.m. silent film performance was a musical organ playing popular tunes of the day. For the children, there was a special session on Saturday mornings at 10.45 a.m. sharp.

153. This picture looking up Fairfield Road is thought to have been taken in 1911 when the Coronation of George V was being celebrated with a traditional display of flags and bunting.

RALPH SMITH,
COMPLETE HOUSE FURNISHER
PHONE 16 81·83, HIGH ST·BRAINTREE.

BRAINTREE CARNIVAL. 1924.   16.   BULL. Photo.

154. In earlier days local carnivals were major events in the social life of a small town and Braintree was no exception. Here, at the Braintree carnival procession in 1924, Ralph Smith stands proudly besides a lorry advertising his shop.

155. Attending the same procession was this motor float advertising Sun Maid, a well-known product at the time.

156. The 750th anniversary of the founding of Braintree was celebrated with much enthusiasm in 1949. Among the events was a street procession with Miss Braintree (Ruby Archer) escorted around the town by boys in period costume.

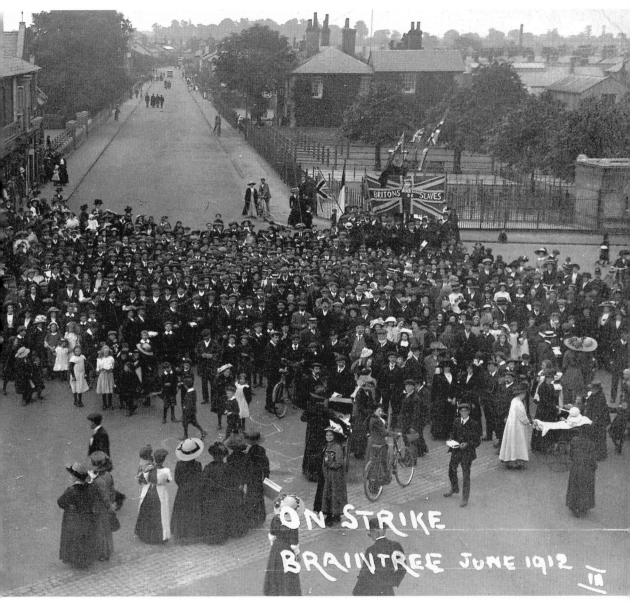

On the banner: BRITONS NEVER BE SLAVES

ON STRIKE
BRAINTREE JUNE 1912

57. The attitude of industrialists to the people in Braintree was of benign paternalism. Nevertheless, it was inevitable that
sputes would arise, leading to the workers making use of their ultimate weapon—strike. In June 1912, a meeting demanding
tion was held in Market Place.

158. At the turn of the century Henry Joscelyne moved the entire contents of Skreens Hall, Roxwell, in 44 van loads for his client, the Earl of Arran. It was his largest commission.

159. A copy of Benjamin Joscelyne's auction schedule of 10 February 1802.

TO BE SOLD BY AUCTION,

By BENJAMIN JOSCELYNE,

On WEDNESDAY next, the 10th of FEBRUARY, 1802

(For the Benefit of the Creditors.)

The Household Furniture & Stock in Trade,

Of Wm. PRATER, Blanket-Maker, BRAINTREE;

Comprising the following useful Articles:

1 LOT of coarse ware	43 Basket, stock cards, and sundries
2 Earthen ware	44 Beam and scales
3 Tea tray, sundry cups, saucers and glasses	45 Eighty-nine lbs. of lead weights
4 Copper saucepan, 2 candlesticks, and box	46 One cwt. 1 qr. 23 lbs. of bloom ditto
5 Knife tray, knives and forks, &c.	47 Quantity of oil, at 4 per gallon
6 Bellows, sifter, and salt box	48 Two dozen old cards
7 Fire pan, poker, tongs, and fender	49 Ditto
8 Crane, hooks, and trivet	50 One blanket wrapper
9 Coal grates	51 Ditto
10 Wainscot bureau	52 Ditto
11 Wainscot tea table	53 Two setts of blanket tackling
12 Oval table	54 Ditto
13 Large ditto	55 Ditto
14 Six wicker-bottom'd chairs	56 Winding wheel and swift
15 A thirty-hour'd clock, on bracket	57 A broad loom, complete
16 Pier glass, in gilt frame	58 Four blanket thirtles
17 Chest of drawers	59 A gig mill
18 Large hutch	60 Large ditto
19 Folding board and supporters	61 Box scrave and perch
20 Arm chair and 1 other ditto	62 Winding wheel, stool and swift
21 Roasting jack	63 Long form and sorting board
22 Brass kettle and furnace	64 Basket, pair of stock cards, & 2 pair of shears
23 Two small wash tubs	65 Sack, with wool, cotton, &c.
24 Stool, tub, and firkin	66 Warping bars and scailet
25 Painted rain-water tub, and brass tap	67 Four dozen bobbins
26 Tub, stool, &c.	68 One dozen new cards
27 Nine elm quarters, and 1 beam	69 84 lbs. of baize yarn, 14 bundles
28 Iron-bound hogshead cask	70 84 lbs. of blanket wool, 12 ditto
29 Ditto	71 116 lbs. of warp yarn, 17 ditto
30 Half-hogshead ditto	72 34 lbs. of fine grey yarn, 6 ditto
31 Ditto	73 44 lbs. of coloured ditto, 5 ditto
32 Two beer stalls	74 85 lbs. of mantling ditto, 18 ditto
33 The pig's cot, and some spray	75 6 lbs. of dy'd ditto
34 Lot of dung	76 72 lbs. of fine grey ditto
35 A bedstead	77 Quantity of ground wool, at 19 per lb.
36 Sundries	78 Ditto ordinary
37 Ditto	79 Ditto broad head
38 Ditto	80 Ditto middle wool
39 Ditto	81 Ditto coloured locks
40 Ditto	82 A 10-4 tenter, as it stands
	83 An 8 4 ditto
Stock in Trade.	84 Ditto
41 Tin kettle, strainer, and pint pot	85 Rack iron and bar
42 The wool bin, as fixed	86

Sale will begin at ELEVEN o'Clock.

SHEARCROFT, PRINTER, BOCKING.

160. The Rivers Pant and Brain have always been liable to overflow in times of excessive rainfall. In 1903, Church Street, Bocking, was severely flooded and work at Courtaulds was disrupted.

FLOOD CHURCH ST

161. On 1 March 1952 the last passenger train to Bishop's Stortford arrives at Braintree railway station; its engine has clearly seen better days. Steam engines continued to use the line between Braintree and Witham until they were replaced by diesel locos in the late 1950s.

162. The 1931 wedding of Ivy and Ron Hales, with their parents and bridesmaid, Joan Butcher outside Belgravia Villas, Church Street, Bocking. Like so many townspeople, Ron was employed by Courtaulds.

The People

163. Sir William Julien Courtauld J.P. was, like other members of his family, a substantial benefactor to the town. In 1921 he was responsible for the construction of the present hospital in London Road, whilst in 1928 he built and presented the old Town Hall to the community. It remained the seat of local government until 1974. It is now the Tourist Centre. He also donated the fountain and Nurses' Homes next to St Michael's church.

164. Lord Braintree, Valentine Crittall (1884-1961) was a prominent figure in the area, both as Chairman of the Crittall Manufacturing Company Ltd., and as a public figure. In 1923 he was elected Labour M.P. for the Maldon constituency (which included Braintree), was knighted in 1931 and was elevated to the peerage in 1947.

165 & 166. Mr. W. B. Lake in 1892 established a firm in New Street for the manufacture of cycle parts, at first employing three or four men. Later he was joined by Mr. E. F. Elliot and in premises known as Albion Works (illustration 75) the firm rapidly expanded, specialising in making tools and parts for bicycles and for the embryonic motor car industry.

167. Office Staff at Lake & Elliot, *c.*1920.

168. The much loved Dr. 'Jack' Harrison (1857-1929) with his two pet Sealyhams and friend. Dr. Harrison lived in Bank Street with a strange island garden in the centre of the road. Although a dedicated doctor, he had an irrepressible sense of fun and his pranks are legion. He had the habit of preparing his bills to patients once a year, but those for the old or poor were never delivered.

169. Braintree's small police contingent gathers outside the premises at Rayne Road, *c*.1860. By 1888 the size of the force for the Braintree Division had grown to 35 officers.

170. Braintree's police force outside the Fairfield Road Station in 1907. In the centre is Superintendent George Terry.

171. Unlike most firms in the 19th century, Courtaulds employed large numbers of women. Many were recruited locally but others migrated from Bow and Spitalfields. Pictured here, *c*.1859, are a group of silk sorters and their male overseer.

172. Mrs. Cooper, the wife of a well-known local businessman, and her children, Leslie and Winnie, *c*.1900. Winnie went on to marry Lawrence Goodwin and became a well-known dog exhibitor.

173. This group photograph shows the Braintree & West Essex Co-operative Society's Women's Guild Committee in 1914.

174. The 1928 silver wedding photograph of the Archer family. In the centre are Charles and Gertrude Archer.

175. The wedding photograph of Hilda Hind and Charles Brown with best man Gordon Day and bridesmaids (*left*) Marion Davies, (*centre*) Kathleen Reed and (*right*) Elaine Joslin in the porch of St Michael's church on 7 February 1942. Mr. and Mrs. Brown now live at Danbury.

176. Leslie Davies of Chelmsford on his Norton motor bike, *c*.1930. At the time he was an apprentice at Lake & Elliot's. During the week he lodged in Sunnyside.

177. Miss Ruby Archer, who was Miss Braintree in the 750th anniversary celebrations of the founding of Braintree in 1949.

178. Miss Nancy Harris, a member of the Women's Land Army, worked on a local farm delivering milk by pony and trap. On one occasion Polly, the pony, failed to stop at traffic lights and Miss Harris was charged and fined 2s. 6d. by the local bench.

Bibliography

Ashwell, W., *Memories of Dr. John Harrison*, 1970
Baker, Michael, *The Book of Braintree & Bocking*, 1992
Blake, David J., *Window Vision*, 1989
Braintree & Bocking in Old Picture Postcards, Vols. 1, 2 and 3
Branigan, Keith, *Roman Britain*, 1980
Crawley, R. J., etc., *The Years Between*, Vols. I & II, 1984
Edwards, A. C., *A History of Essex*, 1958
E.R.O., *Highways and Byways of Essex*, 1950
Essex County Development Plan 1952, Braintree Section
Essex—The County Handbook, 1960
Industries of the Home Counties Business Review 1888-90
Jarvis, S. M. and Harrison, C. T., *In Search of Essex*
Lake & Elliot Ltd., Souvenir booklet, 1920s
Langley, A., *Hicks Bros Ltd.*, 1991
Lloyd, David, *Historic Towns of East Anglia*, 1989
Lombardelli, C. P., *Branch Lines to Braintree*, 1979
Mills, Geoff R., *Hedingham Omnibuses 1960-85*, 1985
Paye, P., *The Bishop's Stortford, Dunmow & Braintree Branch*, 1981
Quin, W. F., *A History of Braintree & Bocking*, 1981
Scarfe, Norman, *Essex*, 1975
Souvenir Programme of the opening of the Town Hall, May 1928
Swindale, D. L., *Branch Lines to Maldon*, 1977
The Law, including Essex Police Magazine, May 1993
Various issues: *Essex Chronicle, Braintree & Witham Times, Essex Countryside Magazine*
White, William, *History of the County of Essex*, 1848
A Brief History of Braintree, Massachusetts, 1949